PIANO · VOCAL · GUITAR

JACKIE EVANCHO *Dream With Me*

"Lovers" omitted from this publication due to licensing restrictions.

ISBN 978-1-4584-1509-7

HAL•LEONARD® CORPORATION

7777 W. BLUEMOUND RD. P.O. BOX 13819 MILWAUKEE, WI 53213

Visit Hal Leonard Online at
www.halleonard.com

WHEN YOU WISH UPON A STAR

Words by NED WASHINGTON
Music by LEIGH HARLINE

* Recorded a half step higher.

NELLA FANTASIA

Music by ENNIO MORRICONE
Italian Lyrics by CHIARA FERRAU

A MOTHER'S PRAYER

Words and Music by DAVID FOSTER
and CAROLE BAYER SAGER

Female vocal 1: I pray you'll be our eyes and watch us where we go, and help us to be wise in times when we don't

NESSUN DORMA
from TURANDOT

By GIACOMO PUCCINI

Slowly, with freedom

Nes - sun dor - ma! Nes - sun dor - ma!

Tu pu - re, o, Prin - ci - pes - sa, nel - la tua fred - da

stan - za, guar - di le stel - le che tre - ma - no d'a -

* Recorded a half step higher.

ANGEL

Words and Music by
SARAH McLACHLAN

Moderately slow

mp

With pedal

Spend all your time

wait - ing _____ for that sec - ond chance,
straight life; _____ and ev - 'ry - where you turn, _____

for a break that would __ make __ it o - kay. __
there's vul - tures and __ thieves __ at your __ back. __

O MIO BABBINO CARO

Written by DAVID FOSTER
and ERIN TAYLOR FOSTER

Moderately slow, with freedom

With pedal

a tempo

rit.

O mio ba - bi - no ca - ro

mi pia - ce è bel - lo, bel - lo; vo' an -

rit.

a tempo

SOMEWHERE
from WEST SIDE STORY

Lyrics by STEPHEN SONDHEIM
Music by LEONARD BERNSTEIN

* Recorded a half step higher.

ALL I ASK OF YOU

from THE PHANTOM OF THE OPERA

Music by ANDREW LLOYD WEBBER
Lyrics by CHARLES HART
Additional Lyrics by RICHARD STILGOE

OMBRA MAI FU

Written by DAVID FOSTER,
SARA MICHAEL FOSTER and JORDAN FOSTER

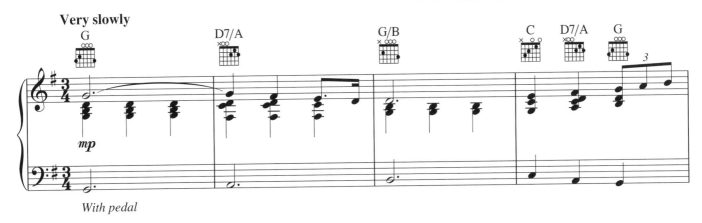

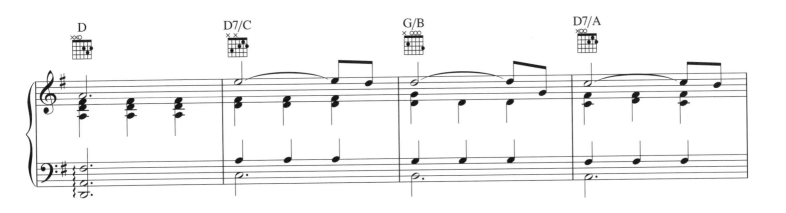

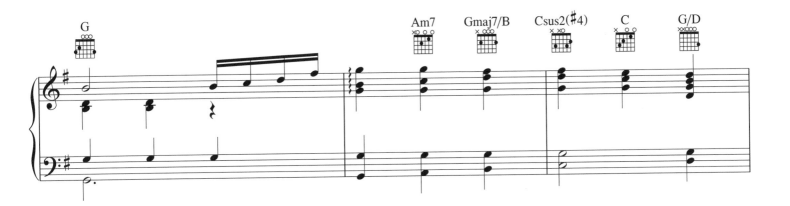

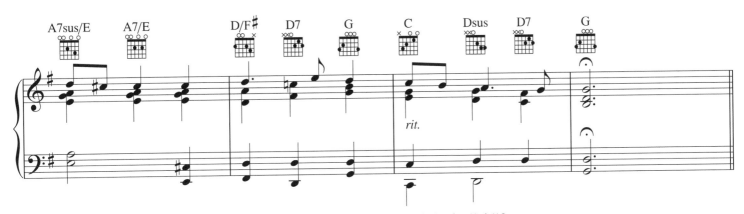

IMAGINER

Words and Music by WALTER AFANASIEFF
and LARA FABIAN

52

c'est d'y croire en - core et mal - gre tout _____ ou - vre les _____

yeux. _____

Instrumental solo

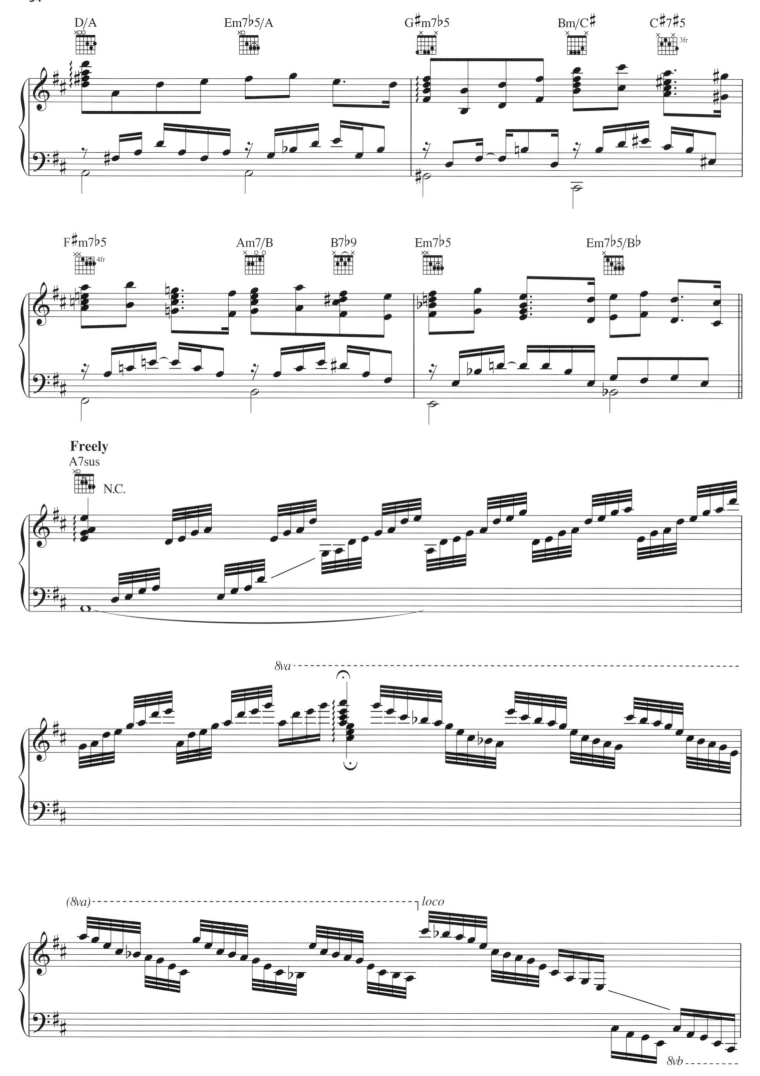

THE LORD'S PRAYER

By ALBERT H. MALOTTE

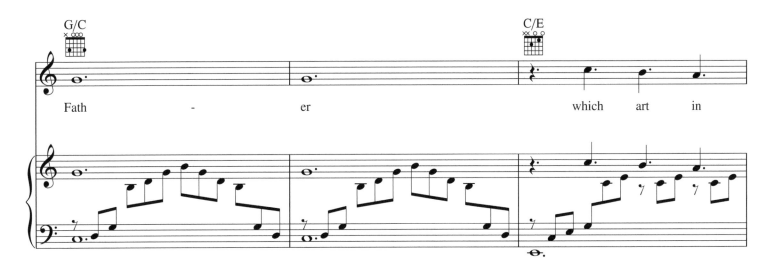

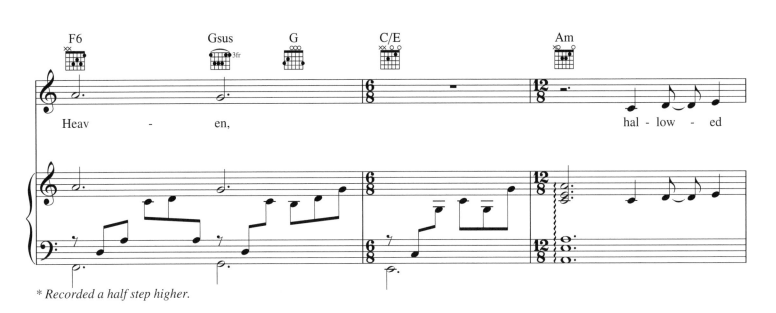

* Recorded a half step higher.

TO BELIEVE

Written by MATTHEW EVANCHO

DREAM WITH ME

Words and Music by JACQUELINE EVANCHO,
DAVID FOSTER and LINDA THOMPSON

Slowly, with feeling

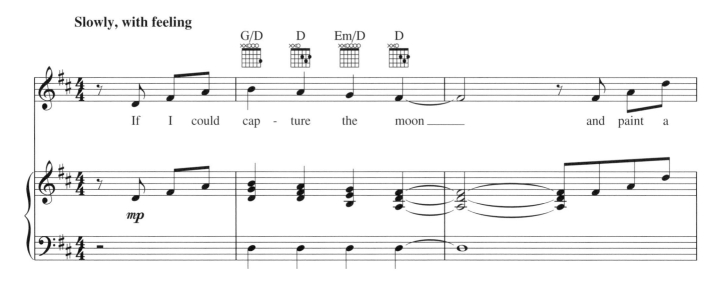

If I could cap-ture the moon ___ and paint a

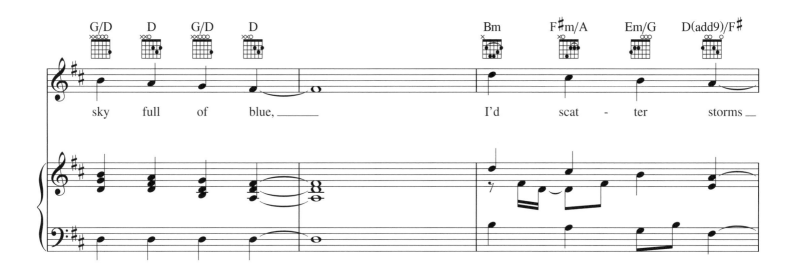

sky full of blue, ___ I'd scat-ter storms ___

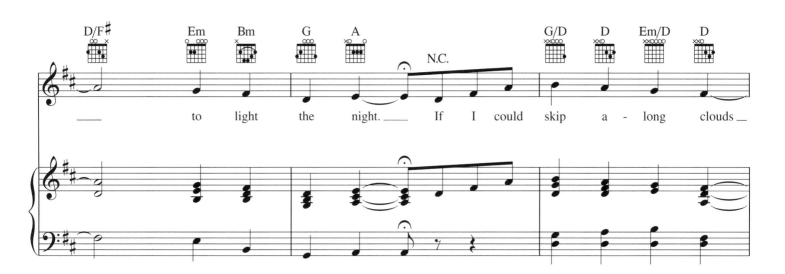

___ to light the night. ___ If I could skip a-long clouds ___